The
Ice-Blue
Bones
of Telluride:

A Dinosaur
Discovery

By Sylvan S. Bald

Illustrations by Ting Taylor

Blue Bones, LLC
Placerville, CO

ISBN: 978-0-692-40503-1
Library of Congress Catalog Card Number: 2015936258
2nd Edition

Printed by Lightning Source, Inc. La Vergne, TN USA 37086.
Printed in the United States of America.
Book Design by Laurie Goralka Design.
Photos by Jeanne Stewart; Ilium Valley photo by Rob Huber.

For more information contact:
Blue Bones, LLC
www.bluebonesllc.com
P.O. Box 451
Placerville, CO 81430

To my Grammy and Grandpa,
Bix and Harold Stewart,
and to all young explorers.

In a small mountain town called
Placerville, Colorado, there lived a boy
named Sylvan. Tall for his age, he had a
mop of dirty blond hair and a skinny frame.
He was a fairly normal kid, besides the fact
that he was homeschooled until seventh grade,
when he enrolled at the Telluride Mountain School.

When he wasn't homeschooling, Sylvan was always outside exploring and building forts. He enjoyed nature and loved building models more than anything. Sylvan would spend hours in his shed carving figures and toy swords from wood. When he couldn't go outside, he would build all kinds of models out of toy bricks in his room.

One fine Thanksgiving morning, Sylvan's parents wanted to go on a family outing. They decided to hike up a dirt trail, which once was an old narrow gauge railroad line that wound around the valley up to the town of Telluride.

The trail went up a long, steep valley called Ilium. That day, fall was in full swing, and the leaves on the trees had turned a deep golden hue.

As they walked along, Sylvan ran
ahead to explore, like he always did.
Sylvan's parents would catch up to
him, and then he'd run ahead again.
They yo-yoed up the trail this way,
until Sylvan rounded a corner.

He glanced down to the left and saw a blue object out of the corner of his eye. He stopped. He looked. He went over to the strange light blue rock. "Are these bones?"

"Why are they blue?" Sylvan pondered to himself. "What were these bones doing embedded in a rock?" He bent down and moved some smaller rocks away from the bigger one, so that he could see the bones more clearly. The big rock was the size of a car tire, while the smaller rocks that had flaked off were the size of an adult hand. The bones were rough and cold to the touch.

Photograph of the actual bones Sylvan discovered.

Sylvan's parents noticed him looking at the peculiar rock and came over to see what was so exciting. As they came up to him, Sylvan said, "Mom, Dad! Look what I just found! I think they're dinosaur bones!" His parents couldn't believe their eyes. They all saw that the bones had been recently exposed by ice cracking off the top layers of rock. Since the bones looked really rare, they all decided to cover them up until the next spring, so that no one else would find the discovery and remove it from the site.

When they got home, Sylvan was very excited. He had many questions about the bones — how did they get there and what type of dinosaur were they from? Sylvan's mom started calling friends to see if they knew of any paleontologists.

A paleontologist is a scientist who studies dinosaur bones and other fossils.

13

She called her friend Linda Luther, who worked for San Miguel County. Ms. Luther contacted the Geology Department at Fort Lewis College in Durango, Colorado. Prof. Jon Powell, Ph.D., a paleontologist from Fort Lewis, wanted to help Sylvan identify the bones' origins. Sylvan and the professor spoke on the phone about the discovery.

"I'm really excited to see the bones." Dr. Powell said. "I've never seen bones that were blue." Sylvan and Dr. Powell agreed that the professor would come to the site in the spring. Until then, Dr. Powell researched the fossilized bones using Ms. Luther's pictures she had taken in the fall.

Then came the long wait. Weeks passed, and spring still hadn't arrived. Snow fell and blanketed the valley and the mountains. The bones were covered up completely with snow, and Sylvan couldn't wait until he could see the fossil again.

Then one day, the sun came out, and the snow melted away, revealing the fossil. It was time to check the bones to determine if they had remained undisturbed.

Ms. Luther scheduled Dr. Powell to come to Telluride
in May to examine the bones. Finally, the day arrived,
and Sylvan was really excited. A big group met at the
discovery site, including Sylvan, his parents, Ms. Luther,
two county employees, a couple of Sylvan's teachers and
Dr. Powell.

When they arrived, Dr. Powell pulled out a bag full of files from his backpack. He examined the bones and then compared them to diagrams of different dinosaur skeletons.

The bones matched almost exactly with one of the images. "Look at this," Dr. Powell said. "They are part of the hip bone known as the ischium belonging to an Allosaurus, a smaller version of the Tyrannosaurus Rex!"

As Sylvan was looking at the bones, he realized he still didn't know why the bones had such an unexpected color. He asked, "Dr. Powell, why are the bones blue?"

"Good question, Sylvan!" Dr. Powell answered. "Let me explain how this happened. After the Allosaurus died, the skeleton lay on the ground for a very long time. Eventually, soil and water covered the bones. During this ancient period, when the bones were fossilizing, or turning into stone, it happened that water carrying the blue-colored mineral, manganese oxide, seeped into the spaces within the bones. When the water left, the mineral stayed, coloring the bones forever. Thank goodness for that mineral, because that is what caught your eye."

"Applying acetone and glue to the bones preserves them during transport."
— Dr. Powell

Once Dr. Powell told everyone at the site about this exciting discovery, he said, "Because these special bones are so valuable, someone could take the bones and sell them. The bones belong in a museum, where everyone can appreciate them. They must be moved to a safe location right away." At that point, Sylvan, his dad and his teachers started making preparations to move the bones to a secure place until Sylvan and his family could determine where this unique find could be placed on permanent display.

Sylvan rode his bike up the trail about a mile to his dad's truck to get moving blankets and other padding to protect the bones.

His dad rented a wheelbarrow to carry them back up the hill.

Meanwhile, Dr. Powell, Ms. Luther, her assistants and his mom helped to clear the area of debris so that the bones could be lifted into the wheelbarrow.

21

When Sylvan, his dad and the teachers returned to the site, they tried lifting the fossilized bones—but the rock was heavy!

In all, it took four people to lift the large rock, and the whole group to push the wheelbarrow up the hill to the cars.

They unloaded the bones into Sylvan's parents' car.

Ms. Luther, Sylvan's parents and Dr. Powell drove into Telluride, where the fossil was secretly stored.

That night during dinner, Sylvan and his parents thought about where the bones could be displayed. They couldn't decide. While Sylvan was sleeping, he had a dream. He dreamt that the bones were being unveiled at the local museum and Sylvan was shaking hands with the mayor. There were balloons and confetti, and a huge party was being held in Sylvan's honor.

Sylvan's mom contacted officials at the museum to see if they would like to exhibit the bones. The museum director realized that Sylvan's discovery included the first bones to be found in the Telluride area. The director said she was excited to have the fossils, but the museum needed a special protective case, which was very expensive. Everyone would have to wait until the museum could raise enough money for it.

The next morning, Sylvan told his parents that he wanted to put the bones in the local museum — the Telluride Historical Museum.

Fossil Exhibit: Grand Opening

Another long wait came while the museum raised money.
During that time, Sylvan instructed some younger students
at his school. He showed them the fossilized bones, let
them display the bones in one of their class projects and
took them on a hike down to where the fossil was found.
The kids were thrilled to be able to see real dinosaur
bones, and they thought it was really cool that an older
student had found them.

Finally, the day came when the museum opened the exhibit of Sylvan's discovery, the fossil. It was a very exciting day for many people, especially Sylvan. If it hadn't been for his careful eye, this fossil may have never been found and appreciated by everyone who comes to the museum to learn about our ancient past.

So, next time you are outside exploring, keep your eyes open, and maybe you too will find an extraordinary discovery — be it special just for you or for many others.

27

Did you know? The Allosaurus:

- Lived during the late Jurassic period (154-144 million years ago) before the Tyrannosaurus Rex was alive
- Lived in Wyoming, Utah and Colorado — also in Spain, Russia and Africa
- Was a carnivore (ate large plant-eating dinosaurs such as Stegosaurus, Iguanodon and Apatosaurus)
- Had little biting power (less than a lion, alligator or leopard) but made up for it by using its head like an axe and driving its upper jaw into its prey

- Could lose its 4-inch-long teeth and grow new ones like a shark
- Was named Allosaurus for the Latin name "other lizard" — early finds showed that their bones were different from those of other dinosaurs of that time

- Had two bony horns in front of the eyes and two lumps behind them — which may have been used to shade the eyes, for identification, or for mating selection
- Was 12 meters long (the length of a school bus)

- Grew to be 5 meters high (like a two story building)
- Weighed up 2 tons (as much as a midsize car)
- Ribs grew from its belly skin rather than from the backbone

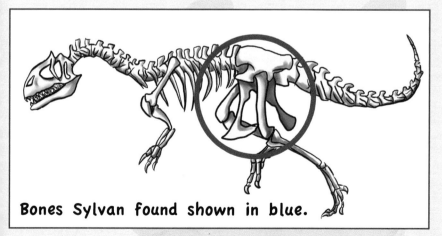

Bones Sylvan found shown in blue.

- Used its short arms for grabbing its prey
- Was not a strong biped (two-legged) runner, with a top speed of only 21 mph

(from different web sources)

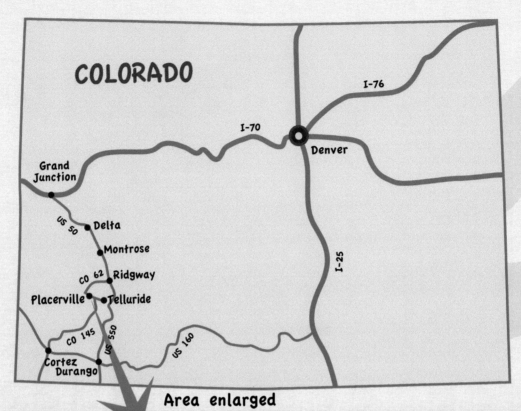

COLORADO

I-76

I-70

Denver

I-25

Grand
Junction

US 50

Delta

Montrose

CO 62

Ridgway

Placerville

Telluride

CO 145

US 550

US 160

Cortez
Durango

Area enlarged

Placerville

Sawpit

San Miguel River

Mountain Village

Telluride

Ilium Valley

N

NOT TO SCALE

Courtesy San Miguel County GIS

Thank you to the following people who helped make this book possible from the time Sylvan found the bones until Sylvan and Ting wrote, illustrated and published the book.

Linda Luther and the San Miguel County Open Space and Recreation staff for helping get the bones to a safe place and holding them until the museum was ready for the new addition.

Dr. Jon Powell, Ph.D., of Fort Lewis College, Durango, CO, for his expertise in determining that the blue bones belonged to an Allosaurus and for deftly explaining the fossilizing process of the blue bones.

Erica Kinias and staff of the Telluride Historical Museum, for funding and obtaining the special case to preserve the bones and safely showcase them for all to see in the future.

Pamela Lifton-Zoline of the Telluride Institute, who motivated Sylvan and Ting to create the book and who gave literary and artistic (and financial) support to both Sylvan and Ting all along the way.

Jesse James McTigue of the Telluride Mountain School, who helped Sylvan start writing the book, and who gave him feedback and ideas to sharpen the flow of the book.

Renee Stewart, auntie extraordinaire, of Chanhassen, MN who edited the book on a deadline and gave Sylvan some great ideas and support.

Laurie Goralka Casselberry, of Laurie Goralka Design in Durango, CO, who designed the book while teaching us so much about the publishing world and helping us make deadlines.

Sylvan and Ting thank their respective parents – Jeanne Stewart and Ian Bald, and Billi and Lee Taylor – for their guidance, support, and deadline enforcement.

And Deb D'Angelo, Daiva Chesonis and David Holbrooke, who all advised about publishing realities and helped with other significant areas of getting the book published and out into the community and world for others to read...

Born in Washington, D.C. in 1998, Sylvan moved back to Placerville, CO, with his parents when he was two months old. Throughout his childhood, Sylvan spent a lot of time outside exploring the woods, the rock cliffs and the old town dump near the family's home. Here was where his love for adventure and finding interesting objects of all kinds flourished. As a homeschooler until seventh grade, Sylvan learned to appreciate the planet as his classroom. His family spent a lot of time learning about the world through reading, traveling and diving into interesting subjects. When Sylvan is not finding new treasures wherever he goes, he loves skiing, running, reading, traveling — especially to northern Minnesota to spend time at the family cabin — and doing art work. He hopes to continue his education through new adventures wherever he goes.

Ting arrived from Fujian Province (福建) in December of 1998, to the family homestead in Fall Creek, a mere two miles upstream from Sylvan and his family. The two families — and Ting and Sylvan — became fast friends. Not surprisingly, Sylvan and Ting's early childhood ambition was to open a dinosaur museum and animal ranch together in Placerville...

Ting began to draw as soon as she could hold any sort of writing utensil, and simply never stopped. While traveling with her parents in her early years, she filled numerous notebooks with drawings of unique creatures and of dinosaurs. Since then, her subject matter evolved to dragons and cat clans, wolves, and character studies. Ting now hones her skills at digital animation and plans to attend college with a focus on the digital arts. When not drawing, animating, or studying, Ting listens to music and plays for the Telluride High School on the Miners soccer team.

CPSIA information can be obtained
at www.ICGtesting.com
Printed in the USA
LVIC04n0332110915
453568LV00001B/2

9 780692 405031